ME TOO!®
B O O K S

GOD, PLEASE SEND FIRE!

ELIJAH AND THE PROPHETS OF BAAL

By Marilyn Lashbrook

Illustrated by Chris Sharp

RAINBOW
STUDIES
INTERNATIONAL

El Reno, Oklahoma

Creating Colorful Treasures™

ME TOO!® Books are designed to
help you share the joy of reading
with children. They provide a new
and fun way to improve a child's
reading skills — by practice and
example. At the same time, you
are teaching your child valuable
Bible truths.

GOD, PLEASE SEND FIRE assures
your child that there is only one
true and powerful God who hears
and answers prayer. This book
opens the door for you to discuss
who God is, how he differs from other
gods, and why we worship Him.

Reading is the key to successful
education. Obeying the principles
of God's Word opens the door to a
successful life. **ME TOO!**® Books
encourage your children in both!

Bold type: Child reads.
Regular type: Adult reads.

   Wait for child to respond.

   Talk about it!

Library of Congress Catalog Card Number: 90-60458
ISBN 0-933657-79-X

Art direction and design by
Chris Schechner Graphic Design.

1 2 3 4 5 6 7 8 9 — 02 01 00 99
Rainbow Studies International, El Reno, OK 73036, U.S.A.

GOD, PLEASE SEND FIRE!

ELIJAH AND THE PROPHETS OF BAAL

Taken from 1 Kings 17-18

Elijah, the prophet of God had bad news for King Ahab. "It will not rain again for years!" Elijah said. "Not until I say so."

Then God told Elijah to go and hide. King Ahab was angry enough to kill him.

As the days and weeks went by, the grass died, the flowers withered and thirsty animals hunted for water.

The people were thirsty and hungry. They were dirty too, because there had been no rain for three years. That's a long time to go without a bath!

King Ahab was thirsty too. No water to brush his teeth. No water to wash his feet. Phew! Stinky Poo!

But God kept Elijah safe and provided him with water. One day God sent His prophet to meet King Ahab.

The king hated Elijah. He blamed him for the drought - the years without rain. But King Ahab knew there would be no rain until Elijah said so.

Clouds of dust rose from the thirsty ground as King Ahab stomped toward Elijah.

"Trouble Maker!" Ahab shouted.

But Elijah replied, "You and your family are the cause of Israel's trouble. You disobey God's commands and teach the people to pray to Baal."

"Now, go!" Elijah said with a wave of his arm, "Send for all the people to meet me on Mount Carmel. And bring the prophets of Baal."

"We will find out whose god is real!"

So King Ahab called everyone to come to Mount Carmel. The prophets of Baal came. King Ahab came. Elijah met them there. And the people watched to see what would happen.

Elijah spoke to the people. "When will you make up your mind?" he asked. "If the Lord is God, worship him. But if Baal is God, follow him."

Nobody spoke a word.

"We will have a contest," Elijah said, "And here are the rules . . ."

"First, the prophets of Baal will build an altar and place a sacrifice on it. "

"But," Elijah said, "no matches! You can't set fire to it. Instead, you must ask Baal to send fire to burn the sacrifice."

"Next, I will build an altar to the True and Living God," Elijah told them. "I will also prepare a sacrifice, but I will pray to the Lord God."

"The God who answers by fire," Elijah thundered, "He is God."

The people agreed. The contest sounded like a good way to find out which God was real. Does it sound like a good idea to you? Why?

"You go first," Elijah said to the false prophets. So they built an altar and prepared a sacrifice. Then they prayed to Baal to send fire.

Nothing happened.

The prophets prayed again...and again...and again. They called on Baal all morning long.

"O Baal," they shouted, "Answer us!"

Still there was no answer.

They danced and they pranced like they had ants in their pants! They shouted. They prayed. But nothing happened. Nothing at all.

At noon, Elijah began to tease them.

"Shout louder!" he suggested

"Maybe Baal is busy!"

"Maybe he's on vacation!"

"Maybe he's asleep!"

So the evil prophets shouted louder and louder. They danced faster and faster. They were frantic.

The afternoon dragged on and still there was no answer. Baal had no power to answer prayers.

When evening came, Elijah called to the people, "Come here!"

The people gathered around Elijah. They watched him lift twelve large stones and stack them together to make an altar. He dug a ditch around it. He placed wood and a sacrifice on the altar.

Then Elijah told the people to pour four buckets of water on the sacrifice. **"Do it again," he said. So they did. "Do it once more!" And they did.**

The water splashed down the sides of the altar and filled the ditch. God's people wondered if a soggy sacrifice could burn. That would be a miracle - something only God could do.

Elijah was not worried. He had faith in God. He knew God's power.

Elijah did not shout.

He did not dance around.

He just prayed to the God he loved.

"O Lord," Elijah prayed, "Let the people know that you are God, and I am Your servant. Answer me so these people will know that you, O Lord, are God."

Would God answer this kind of prayer? ●

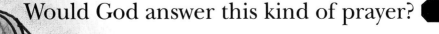

Zap! Fire fell from Heaven and burned

the sacrifice,

and the wood,

and the stones,

and the dust.

It even licked up the water in the ditch.

"The Lord, He is God!"

the people cried out. "The

Lord - He is God!"

The prophets of Baal were taken away. Never again would they teach people to worship Baal.

"There is a big storm coming," Elijah told King Ahab. "Go back home."

Now God could once again bless His people. Big black clouds filled the sky. A strong wind whipped dust and debris into the air.

And then, at last, the heavy raindrops fell. What a day! The drought was over. God had won.

On the way home, the people splashed in the puddles and rejoiced in the Lord, the only true God. ♥♥

ME TOO!®
B O O K S

Ages 2-7

SOMEONE TO LOVE THE STORY OF CREATION	**NO TREE FOR CHRISTMAS** THE STORY OF JESUS' BIRTH
TWO BY TWO THE STORY OF NOAH'S FAITH	**NOW I SEE** THE STORY OF THE MAN BORN BLIND
I DON'T WANT TO THE STORY OF JONAH	**DON'T ROCK THE BOAT** THE STORY OF THE MIRACULOUS CATCH
I MAY BE LITTLE THE STORY OF DAVID'S GROWTH	**OUT ON A LIMB** THE STORY OF ZACCHAEUS
I'LL PRAY ANYWAY THE STORY OF DANIEL	**SOWING AND GROWING** THE PARABLE OF THE SOWER AND THE SOILS
WHO NEEDS A BOAT? THE STORY OF MOSES	**DON'T STOP. . . FILL EVERY POT** THE STORY OF THE WIDOW'S OIL
GET LOST, LITTLE BROTHER THE STORY OF JOSEPH	**GOOD, BETTER, BEST** THE STORY OF MARY AND MARTHA
THE WALL THAT DID NOT FALL THE STORY OF RAHAB'S FAITH	**GOD'S HAPPY HELPERS** THE STORY OF TABITHA AND FRIENDS

Ages 5-10

IT'S NOT MY FAULT MAN'S BIG MISTAKE	**NOTHING TO FEAR** JESUS WALKS ON WATER	**NOBODY KNEW BUT GOD** MIRIAM AND BABY MOSES
GOD, PLEASE SEND FIRE ELIJAH AND THE PROPHETS OF BAAL	**THE BEST DAY EVER** THE STORY OF JESUS	**MORE THAN BEAUTIFUL** THE STORY OF ESTHER
TOO BAD, AHAB NABOTH'S VINEYARD	**THE GREAT SHAKE-UP** MIRACLES IN PHILIPPI	**FAITH TO FIGHT** THE STORY OF CALEB
THE WEAK STRONGMAN SAMSON	**TWO LADS AND A DAD** THE PRODIGAL SON	**BIG ENEMY, BIGGER GOD** THE STORY OF GIDEON

WE SEE!™
V I D E O S
VIDEOS FOR TODAY'S CHRISTIAN FAMILY.
*51 animated Bible stories from the Old Testament ("In the Beginning" Series) and
New Testament ("A Kingdom without Frontiers" Series) will provide your children
with a solid cornerstone of spiritual support.*

Available at your local bookstore or from:

Rainbow Studies International • P.O. Box 759 • El Reno, Oklahoma 73036

1-800-242-5348

RSI
Creating Colorful Treasures™